THE JPS B'NAI MITZVAH TORAH COMMENTARY

Va-yeḥi (Genesis 47:28–50:26)
Haftarah (1 Kings 2:1–12)

Rabbi Jeffrey K. Salkin

The Jewish Publication Society · Philadelphia
University of Nebraska Press · Lincoln

INTRODUCTION

News flash: the most important thing about becoming bar or bat mitzvah isn't the party. Nor is it the presents. Nor even being able to celebrate with your family and friends—as wonderful as those things are. Nor is it even standing before the congregation and reading the prayers of the liturgy—as important as that is.

No, the most important thing about becoming bar or bat mitzvah is sharing Torah with the congregation. And why is that? Because of all Jewish skills, that is the most important one.

Here is what is true about rites of passage: you can tell what a culture values by the tasks it asks its young people to perform on their way to maturity. In American culture, you become responsible for driving, responsible for voting, and yes, responsible for drinking responsibly.

In some cultures, the rite of passage toward maturity includes some kind of trial, or a test of strength. Sometimes, it is a kind of "outward bound" camping adventure. Among the Maasai tribe in Africa, it is traditional for a young person to hunt and kill a lion. In some Hispanic cultures, fifteen year-old girls celebrate the *quinceañera*, which marks their entrance into maturity.

What is Judaism's way of marking maturity? It combines both of these rites of passage: *responsibility* and *test*. You show that you are on your way to becoming a *responsible* Jewish adult through a public *test* of strength and knowledge—reading or chanting Torah, and then teaching it to the congregation.

This is the most important Jewish ritual mitzvah (commandment), and that is how you demonstrate that you are, truly, bar or bat mitzvah—old enough to be responsible for the mitzvot.

What Is Torah?

So, what exactly is the Torah? You probably know this already, but let's review.

The Torah (teaching) consists of "the five books of Moses," sometimes also called the *chumash* (from the Hebrew word *chameish,* which means "five"), or, sometimes, the Greek word Pentateuch (which means "the five teachings").

Here are the five books of the Torah, with their common names and their Hebrew names.

> **Genesis (The beginning), which in Hebrew is Bere'shit (from the first words—"When God began to create").** Bere'shit spans the years from Creation to Joseph's death in Egypt. Many of the Bible's best stories are in Genesis: the creation story itself; Adam and Eve in the Garden of Eden; Cain and Abel; Noah and the Flood; and the tales of the Patriarchs and Matriarchs, Abraham, Isaac, Jacob, Sarah, Rebekah, Rachel, and Leah. It also includes one of the greatest pieces of world literature, the story of Joseph, which is actually the oldest complete novel in history, comprising more than one-quarter of all Genesis.

> **Exodus (Getting out), which in Hebrew is Shemot (These are the names).** Exodus begins with the story of the Israelite slavery in Egypt. It then moves to the rise of Moses as a leader, and the Israelites' liberation from slavery. After the Israelites leave Egypt, they experience the miracle of the parting of the Sea of Reeds (or "Red Sea"); the giving of the Ten Commandments at Mount Sinai; the idolatry of the Golden Calf; and the design and construction of the Tabernacle and of the ark for the original tablets of the law, which our ancestors carried with them in the desert. Exodus also includes various ethical and civil laws, such as "You shall not wrong a stranger or oppress him, for you were strangers in the land of Egypt" (22:20).

> **Leviticus (about the Levites), or, in Hebrew, Va-yikra' (And God called).** It goes into great detail about the kinds of sacrifices that the ancient Israelites brought as offerings; the laws of ritual purity; the animals that were permitted and forbidden for eating (the beginnings of the tradition of kashrut, the Jewish dietary laws); the diagnosis of various skin diseases; the ethical laws of holiness; the ritual calendar of the Jewish year; and various agricultural laws concerning the treatment of the Land of Israel. Leviticus is basically the manual of ancient Judaism.

> Numbers (because the book begins with the census of the Israelites), or, in Hebrew, Be-midbar (In the wilderness). The book describes the forty years of wandering in the wilderness and the various rebellions against Moses. The constant theme: "Egypt wasn't so bad. Maybe we should go back." The greatest rebellion against Moses was the negative reports of the spies about the Land of Israel, which discouraged the Israelites from wanting to move forward into the land. For that reason, the "wilderness generation" must die off before a new generation can come into maturity and finish the journey.

> Deuteronomy (The repetition of the laws of the Torah), or, in Hebrew, Devarim (The words). The final book of the Torah is, essentially, Moses's farewell address to the Israelites as they prepare to enter the Land of Israel. Here we find various laws that had been previously taught, though sometimes with different wording. Much of Deuteronomy contains laws that will be important to the Israelites as they enter the Land of Israel—laws concerning the establishment of a monarchy and the ethics of warfare. Perhaps the most famous passage from Deuteronomy contains the *Shema*, the declaration of God's unity and uniqueness, and the *Ve-ahavta*, which follows it. Deuteronomy ends with the death of Moses on Mount Nebo as he looks across the Jordan Valley into the land that he will not enter.

Jews read the Torah in sequence—starting with Bere'shit right after Simchat Torah in the autumn, and then finishing Devarim on the following Simchat Torah. Each Torah portion is called a parashah (division; sometimes called a *sidrah*, a place in the order of the Torah reading). The stories go around in a full circle, reminding us that we can always gain more insights and more wisdom from the Torah. This means that if you don't "get" the meaning this year, don't worry—it will come around again.

And What Else? The Haftarah

We read or chant the Torah from the Torah scroll—the most sacred thing that a Jewish community has in its possession. The Torah is written without vowels, and the ability to read it and chant it is part of the challenge and the test.

But there is more to the synagogue reading. Every Torah reading has an accompanying haftarah reading. Haftarah means "conclusion," because there was once a time when the service actually ended with that reading. Some scholars believe that the reading of the haftarah originated at a time when non-Jewish authorities outlawed the reading of the Torah, and the Jews read the haftarah sections instead. In fact, in some synagogues, young people who become bar or bat mitzvah read very little Torah and instead read the entire haftarah portion.

The haftarah portion comes from the Nevi'im, the prophetic books, which are the second part of the Jewish Bible. It is either read or chanted from a Hebrew Bible, or maybe from a booklet or a photocopy.

The ancient sages chose the haftarah passages because their themes reminded them of the words or stories in the Torah text. Sometimes, they chose *haftarah* with special themes in honor of a festival or an upcoming festival.

Not all books in the prophetic section of the Hebrew Bible consist of prophecy. Several are historical. For example:

The book of Joshua tells the story of the conquest and settlement of Israel.

The book of Judges speaks of the period of early tribal rulers who would rise to power, usually for the purpose of uniting the tribes in war against their enemies. Some of these leaders are famous: Deborah, the great prophetess and military leader, and Samson, the biblical strong man.

The books of Samuel start with Samuel, the last judge, and then move to the creation of the Israelite monarchy under Saul and David (approximately 1000 BCE).

The books of Kings tell of the death of King David, the rise of King Solomon, and how the Israelite kingdom split into the Northern Kingdom of Israel and the Southern Kingdom of Judah (approximately 900 BCE).

And then there are the books of the prophets, those spokesmen for God whose words fired the Jewish conscience. Their names are immortal: Isaiah, Jeremiah, Ezekiel, Amos, Hosea, among others.

Someone once said: "There is no evidence of a biblical prophet ever being invited back a second time for dinner." Why? Because the prophets were tough. They had no patience for injustice, apathy, or hypocrisy. No one escaped their criticisms. Here's what they taught:

› God commands the Jews to behave decently toward one another. In fact, God cares more about basic ethics and decency than about ritual behavior.
› God chose the Jews *not* for special privileges, but for special duties to humanity.
› As bad as the Jews sometimes were, there was always the possibility that they would improve their behavior.
› As bad as things might be now, it will not always be that way. Someday, there will be universal justice and peace. Human history is moving forward toward an ultimate conclusion that some call the Messianic Age: a time of universal peace and prosperity for the Jewish people and for all the people of the world.

Your Mission—To Teach Torah to the Congregation

On the day when you become bar or bat mitzvah, you will be reading, or chanting, Torah—in Hebrew. You will be reading, or chanting, the haftarah—in Hebrew. That is the major skill that publicly marks the becoming of bar or bat mitzvah. But, perhaps even more important than that, you need to be able to teach something about the Torah portion, and perhaps the haftarah as well.

And that is where this book comes in. It will be a very valuable resource for you, and your family, in the b'nai mitzvah process.

Here is what you will find in it:

› A brief **summary** of every Torah portion. This is a basic overview of the portion; and, while it might not refer to everything in the Torah portion, it will explain its most important aspects.
› A list of the **major ideas** in the Torah portion. The purpose: to make the Torah portion real, in ways that we can relate to. Every Torah portion contains unique ideas, and when you put all

of those ideas together, you actually come up with a list of Judaism's most important ideas.

> Two **divrei Torah** ("words of Torah," or "sermonettes") for each portion. These *divrei Torah* explain significant aspects of the Torah portion in accessible, reader-friendly language. Each *devar Torah* contains references to **traditional** Jewish sources (those that were written before the modern era), as well as **modern** sources and quotes. We have searched, far and wide, to find sources that are unusual, interesting, and not just the "same old stuff" that many people already know about the Torah portion. Why did we include these minisermons in the volume? Not because we want you to simply copy those sermons and pass them off as your own (that would be cheating), though you are free to quote from them. We included them so that you can see what is possible—how you can try to make meaning for yourself out of the words of Torah.

> **Connections:** This is perhaps the most valuable part. It's a list of questions that you can ask yourself, or that others might help you think about—any of which can lead to the creation of your *devar Torah.*

Note: you don't have to like everything that's in a particular Torah portion. Some aren't that loveable. Some are hard to understand; some are about religious practices that people today might find confusing, and even offensive; some contain ideas that we might find totally outmoded.

But this doesn't have to get in the way. After all, most kids spend a lot of time thinking about stories that contain ideas that modern people would find totally bizarre. Any good medieval fantasy story falls into that category.

And we also believe that, if you spend just a little bit of time with those texts, you can begin to understand what the author was trying to say.

This volume goes one step further. Sometimes, the haftarah comes off as a second thought, and no one really thinks about it. We have tried to solve that problem by including a **summary** of each haftarah, and then a mini-sermon on the haftarah. This will help you learn how these sacred words are relevant to today's world, and even to your own life.

All Bible quotations come from the NJPS translation, which is found in the many different editions of the JPS TANAKH; in the Conservative movement's *Etz Hayim: Torah and Commentary;* in the Reform movement's *Torah: A Modern Commentary;* and in other Bible commentaries and study guides.

How Do I Write a *Devar Torah?*

It really is easier than it looks.

There are many ways of thinking about the *devar Torah*. It is, of course, a short sermon on the meaning of the Torah (and, perhaps, the haftarah) portion. It might even be helpful to think of the *devar Torah* as a "book report" on the portion itself.

The most important thing you can know about this sacred task is: *Learn* the words. *Love* the words. Teach people what it could mean to *live* the words.

Here's a basic outline for a *devar Torah:*

"My Torah portion is (name of portion)_____,
   from the book of _____, chapter
   _____.

"In my Torah portion, we learn that_____
   (Summary of portion)
"For me, the most important lesson of this Torah portion is (what
   is the best thing in the portion? Take the portion as a whole;
   your *devar Torah* does not have to be only, or specifically, on the
   verses that you are reading).
"As I learned my Torah portion, I found myself wondering:
   ➤ *Raise a question that the Torah portion itself raises.*
   ➤ *"Pick a fight"* with the portion. Argue with it.
   ➤ *Answer a question* that is listed in the "Connections" section of
      each Torah portion.
   ➤ *Suggest a question to your rabbi* that you would want the rabbi
      to answer in his or her own *devar Torah* or sermon.

"I have lived the values of the Torah by _____
(here, you can talk about how the Torah portion relates to your
own life. If you have done a mitzvah project, you can talk about
that here).

How To Keep It from Being Boring
(and You from Being Bored)

Some people just don't like giving traditional speeches. From our per-
spective, that's really okay. Perhaps you can teach Torah in a different
way—one that makes sense to you.

> Write an "open letter" to one of the characters in your Torah por-
  tion. "Dear Abraham: I hope that your trip to Canaan was not too
  hard . . ." "Dear Moses: Were you afraid when you got the Ten
  Commandments on Mount Sinai? I sure would have been . . ."
> Write a news story about what happens. Imagine yourself to
  be a television or news reporter. "Residents of neighboring cities were horrified yesterday as the wicked cities of Sodom and
  Gomorrah were burned to the ground. Some say that God was
  responsible . . ."
> Write an imaginary interview with a character in your Torah portion.
> Tell the story from the point of view of another character, or a mi-
  nor character, in the story. For instance, tell the story of the Gar-
  den of Eden from the point of view of the serpent. Or the story
  of the Binding of Isaac from the point of view of the ram, which
  was substituted for Isaac as a sacrifice. Or perhaps the story of
  the sale of Joseph from the point of view of his coat, which was
  stripped off him and dipped in a goat's blood.
> Write a poem about your Torah portion.
> Write a song about your Torah portion.
> Write a play about your Torah portion, and have some friends act
  it out with you.
> Create a piece of artwork about your Torah portion.

The bottom line is: Make this a joyful experience. Yes—it could
even be fun.

The Very Last Thing You Need to Know at This Point

The Torah scroll is written without vowels. Why? Don't *sofrim* (Torah scribes) know the vowels?

Of course they do.

So, why do they leave the vowels out?

One reason is that the Torah came into existence at a time when sages were still arguing about the proper vowels, and the proper pronunciation.

But here is another reason: The Torah text, as we have it today, and as it sits in the scroll, is actually *an unfinished work*. Think of it: the words are just sitting there. Because they have no vowels, it is as if they have no voice.

When we read the Torah publicly, we give voice to the ancient words. And when we find meaning in those ancient words, and we talk about those meanings, those words jump to life. They enter our lives. They make our world deeper and better.

Mazal tov to you, and your family. This is your journey toward Jewish maturity. Love it.

THE TORAH

❖ Va-yeḥi: Genesis 47:28–50:26

As we come to the end of the book of Genesis, it is truly a time of transition. Two people die: Jacob, and then his beloved son Joseph. Joseph's brothers worry that, with their father dead, all the old family fights will start up again. But Joseph makes them feel better about the way that everything worked out.

As Genesis ends, the children of Jacob are living, happily and comfortably, in the land of Goshen in Egypt. But, as we shall see, "happily" does not mean "happily ever after."

Summary

> ‣ Jacob, on his deathbed, blesses his grandsons, Ephraim and Manasseh, and then he blesses each of his sons. Each son's blessing refers not only to his character and personality, but also to the destiny of the tribe that will descend from him. When Jacob finishes blessing his sons, he dies. (48:1–49:33)

> ‣ Joseph and his brothers take their father, Jacob, back to Canaan for burial, and then they return to Egypt. (50:1–14)

> ‣ Joseph's brothers are afraid that Joseph will now hate them for what they did to him when he was young. Joseph reassures them, however, and tells them that what has happened was all been part of God's plan for him and his family. (50:15–21)

> ‣ As Joseph is about to die, he makes his brothers swear that, when they finally leave Egypt, his bones will be buried in the Land of Israel. (50:22–26)

The Big Ideas

> **Jacob's blessings of his sons predict the future.** Jacob's words
> to them refer to their personalities, but, even more so, to the fu-
> ture of the tribes that will descend from them. Jacob's blessings
> even foresee the future of the territories in the Land of Israel that
> the tribes will inhabit. A traditional explanation is that God gave
> Jacob the gift of prophecy. Modern scholars would say that the
> blessings—and in a few cases, curses—reflect the realities of Isra-
> elite tribal history.

> **Judaism accepts the reality of bodily death.** When Jacob dies, the
> Egyptians embalm his body, as they do also with Joseph's body.
> This is the well-known practice of mummification. The ancient
> Egyptians believed that the body needed to be preserved in order
> to be reunited with the soul in the afterlife. By contrast, Judaism
> embraces the finality of the body's death, and does not believe
> that it needs to be artificially preserved.

> **The Diaspora (places where Jews live outside of Israel) is an
> historical reality for Jews.** When Jacob's sons carry their father's
> body back to the Land of Israel for burial, they could have stayed
> there. But, instead, they return to Egypt. They had gotten very
> comfortable there, and they might even have thought of them-
> selves as Egyptians. In the same way, American Jews tend to think
> of themselves as Americans; Canadian Jews, as Canadians, etc.

> **Forgiveness is a central Jewish value.** Joseph refuses to hold a
> grudge against his brothers. In this way, he demonstrates the
> Jewish attitude toward grudges—it's best not to carry them.

> **The Land of Israel is always precious to the Jew—even in death.**
> Despite the fact that he has lived his entire adult life in Egypt, Jo-
> seph is, at heart, a Jew. That is why he wants to be buried in the
> Land of Israel—which will ultimately happen when the Israelites
> enter the land. Joseph's deathbed wish emphasizes the Jewish
> linkage to the Land of Israel.

Divrei Torah

DON'T HOLD A GRUDGE!

This is going to happen to you.

No matter how popular you are, not everyone in school is going to be your friend. Or even like you. Some will actually dislike you; some might even be mean to you. You might know this already.

You'll go to your thirtieth high school reunion, and maybe you'll run into the people who didn't like you back then. They might come up to you, and hug you, and say, "Wow! It is so great to see you after all these years! You look wonderful! What are you doing now?"

You may be tempted to remind them of all that they did to you, way back then. You might want to accuse them of being hypocrites and phonies. But you won't. You will remember the story of Joseph, and how he says to his brothers that he basically forgives them for what they had done to him. That's because Joseph will not carry a grudge.

Maybe those who mistreated you actually want you to be honest with them (after all, it might help them feel better).

Similarly, Joseph's brothers worry aloud: "What if Joseph still bears a grudge against us?" (50:15).

The sentence starts with the word *lu,* which has several different meanings. The commentator Rashi says: "*Lu* can mean 'please' and 'if only'" (Rashi on Gen. 50:15). Rashi is saying that Joseph's brothers are still afraid and insecure, and they want Joseph to take seriously what they had done to him. They want Joseph to hold them responsible for what they did, and not simply sweep it under the rug.

But Joseph doesn't hate them, or bear a grudge. This is the great life lesson of Joseph. Joseph sees his life as a life with cosmic consequences. Stuff happened to him for a reason. He is sure what the reason is: "God sent me here to save life. Your hands did not sell me into Egypt; God did." Imagine having an attitude like that!

Rabbi Lawrence Kushner thinks that grudges are really like a slow-acting poison. "In very small doses, I will poison myself for the rest of my life. I will carry around the injury you caused me. I will watch it and guard it. But I will never tell you."

We've come to the end of Genesis. Cain killed his brother, Abel.

Isaac and Ishmael reconciled, but never speak to each other. Jacob and Esau reconciled, and they do speak to each other. Joseph and his brothers reconciled, and speak to each other—and, then, Joseph invited them to live with him. Forgiveness is possible. Healing is possible. Family unity is possible.

THE FIRST TIME ANYONE SAID THE SHEMA

Some people have easy lives, or so we think. Not Jacob.

Jacob was lying on his deathbed. In those final moments, he went over his life. Born as a twin, he struggled in the womb with his brother, Esau. He cheated Esau out of his birthright. He stole his brother's blessing. When his brother sought to kill him, he escaped, stopping for the night at Beth El, where he dreamed of a ladder of angels. He wound up with Leah instead of Rachel, then he married Rachel too. He had a wrestling match with a mysterious stranger that left him with a permanent injury and a new name—Israel, the one who struggles with God.

His daughter, Dinah, was raped. His sons reacted violently. They then sold his son Joseph into slavery in Egypt. For many years, Jacob was bereaved. He thought that his son Joseph was dead. And then, when he was already an old man, he learned that Joseph was still alive. He made the long trip down to Egypt to reunite with Joseph. No wonder that when he met Pharaoh he would say his days had been long and hard.

At the end of his life, Jacob was gripped with fear. Perhaps this covenant that exists between him and God, this covenant that is still in its infancy, this covenant that he has sought so hard to fulfill, in his way—perhaps this covenant will die with him.

A midrash says: "When Jacob was dying, he called his twelve sons and said to them: 'Do you have faith in God?' And they said: 'Hear, O Israel [for that was Jacob's other name] the Lord is our God, the Lord is One.' And Jacob died with these words on his lips: 'Blessed be the name of His glorious kingdom for ever and ever.'" It's a lovely tale about the origin of the *Shema*, but, even more, about who the Jews are—a people that has faith in God

Jacob is like any other Jewish parent. He has worries, dreams, and hopes. He wants to pass his values and his faith to his children and his grandchildren. He wants to perpetuate his people and what is most important to him. He knows he will die, but he wants to live on, like his ancestors before him, in the generations that will come.

Continuing the Jewish people is a major responsibility. But how can you do that, especially as a kid? Steven M. Cohen, one of today's wisest Jewish sociologists, states: "Having Jewish friends in childhood (and later in life) is a good way to predict one's future Jewish identity." The best way to start building a Jewish identity and creating the Jewish future is to create a network of Jewish friends: through religious school, youth group, Jewish summer camp, Israel trips—even social media.

The future of the Jewish people starts with you. And it starts today.

Connections

- What would you want your parents to say to you when they bless you?
- Have you ever held a grudge? What examples in world history and Jewish history of grudges can you think of?
- Are the Jews still holding a grudge against the German people for the Holocaust?
- Do you agree that Joseph's brothers wanted to be taken seriously, and perhaps not be forgiven so quickly?
- What do you think was going through the minds of Jacob's sons when he was dying?
- What do you think your parents' Jewish hopes for you are?
- In what way have you inherited Judaism from your own parents and grandparents?
- Do you agree that having Jewish friends is essential to creating a Jewish identity? What other things are important?

THE HAFTARAH

❖ Va-yeḥi: 1 Kings 2:1–12

King David is dying, and he is conveying his final wishes to his son
Solomon, who will succeed him as king. There is a clear link to the Torah portion, in which the Patriarch Jacob is dying, and he blesses each
of his sons, often foretelling their future and the future of the tribes
that will descend from them. We really can't say that David "blesses"
Solomon; more accurately, he gives him a small laundry list of things
that he wants his son to do after he dies—and they aren't exactly the
most pleasant things.

Even though this is not King David's finest hour, let's remember that
he ruled for forty years, and was a leader of great accomplishment. He
unified the tribes and made Jerusalem the capital. He brought the ark
to Jerusalem and laid the foundation for the great Temple that his son
would build. David secured the borders of Israel. According to tradi-
tion the poet-king even authored many of the beautiful Psalms of the
Hebrew Bible. Last but not least, he founded a dynasty, the House of
David, that would rule for generations.

But as the king lies dying, the biblical text does not refer to him as
"King David," but merely as "David," without his title and without
his crown. This teaches us that death comes to everyone, even and
especially kings, and that in the final hour it doesn't matter what title you had. Death makes everyone equal.

Manning Up, David Style

There's an odd expression that men sometimes use with other men:
"Man up." It's a way of saying: "Hey, do what you have to do, and,
while you're at it, show some courage."

That is precisely what King David is saying in this haftarah. He
counsels Solomon to be strong and "to be a man," and to follow God's
commandments and to pay attention to God's laws.

The great king made his share of mistakes, however. None was greater than his affair with Bathsheba and the cover-up he ordered. And just before he dies there is that "hit list"; David then goes through a list of his enemies and friends, and he tells Solomon what the fate of each one should be.

Did David really want the people who may have insulted or opposed him killed? Was he out for revenge, pure and simple? The medieval commentator Isaac Abravanel says: "David wanted Solomon to know how Joab and Shimei had acted against him so that his son would not appoint them to high office." Perhaps David is urging his son to look carefully at a person's character. Or maybe he uses such strong language to teach Solomon about the value of loyalty: to reward those who have been loyal, and to keep an eye on those who have been disloyal.

Like many leaders whose accomplishments are real, David is far from perfect. Shimon Peres, the Israeli statesman, once said: "Not everything King David did on land [fighting battles] or on roofs [spying on Bathsheba bathing, and then sending her husband to die in battle] appears to me to be Judaism!"

But, in fact, one could argue that all of what King David did, the good and the bad, is part of Jewish history even if not the highest ideals of Judaism. David is a human being, who struggles with his passions and his sins. David did own up to at least some of his biggest mistakes. On a smaller scale than the king, we all do what David did. We sometimes let our passions get the best of us; we are vengeful or petty. Yet we love, dream, and do plenty of good. As Rabbi David Wolpe writes: "David is great because of his complexity, not in spite of it. We see ourselves in this man, and we see this man in ourselves."

❖ Notes

❖ Notes

CPSIA information can be obtained
at www.ICGtesting.com
Printed in the USA
LVHW08s0951050818
585984LV00004B/438/P